D1716872

Be a Zillionaire

The Young Zillionaire's Guide to

Distributing Goods and Services

Antoine Wilson

the rosen publishing group's
**rosen
central**

For Tanya, and for Alf Richards.

Published in 2000 by The Rosen Publishing Group, Inc.
29 East 21st Street, New York, NY 10010

Library of Congress Cataloging-in-Publication Data

Wilson, Antoine.
   The young zillionaire's guide to distributing goods and services / by Antoine Wilson. — 1st ed.
      p. cm. — (Be a zillionaire)
   Includes bibliographical references and index.
   Summary: Provides information about distributing goods and services using middlemen, channels, modes of transportation and the Internet.
   ISBN 0-8239-3259-1 (acid-free)
   1. Physical distribution of goods—Juvenile literature.   2. Service industries-Marketing—Juvenile literature. 3. Marketing—Juvenile literature. [1. Physical distri ution of goods. 2. Service industries—Marketing. 3. Marketing.] I. Title. II. Series.
   HF5416.6 .W55 2000
   658.8—dc21   00-00834

Manufactured in the United States of America

TABLE OF CONTENTS

Marketing Channels and Middlemen

Bo's Pumpkin Patch

It was October 29, and Bo's Pumpkin Patch was empty. Pumpkin carving parties had been canceled. Something was up. Climatic disaster? Pumpkin-eating pests? No. This pumpkin outage was the result of a distribution problem.

Bo's Pumpkin Patch got its pumpkins from Jo Produce, a regional distributor that got its pumpkins from local farmers. The farmers had delivered their crop on schedule, and Jo Produce had paid them.

Soon afterward, the trouble began. Jo Produce's new computer system messed up. Giant produce markets in big cities received a dozen pumpkins, while small towns were inundated with thousands. Bo's Pumpkin Patch eventually received its pumpkins on November 1. It is considerably more difficult to sell pumpkins on November 1st than on October 31! Bo's Pumpkin Patch will use a different distributor next year.

Distribution, Otherwise Known as Marketing

When distribution runs smoothly, it is almost invisible to the consumer. Many of us are aware of distribution only when something goes wrong and we can't get what we want or need. Have you ever gone to the store to purchase something and found it missing from the shelf? Ask salespeople when they expect to have a product back in stock, and they might say that they've put in an order with the distributor. Distributors distribute goods and services. They make sure that the right amount of goods or services gets to the right place, at the right time. If not, the consequences can be disastrous. You could quickly sell two pairs of snowshoes in Alaska in November. Try finding buyers for a hundred pairs of snowshoes in Hawaii in June!

Distribution, known more generally as marketing, is present in almost every aspect of our lives. We live in a consumer-driven society. We want instant and convenient access to products and services. Is there a twenty-four-hour grocery store near you? If not, there will be soon. Is there a McDonald's near your house? The McDonald's corporation wants to have one of their restaurants within four minutes of every American. Even the vending machines at your school are part of an elaborate distribution system.

Distribution is the path taken by goods and services from their origin, as raw materials or manpower, to their final use by the consumer.

There are two major categories of goods: consumer and industrial. Consumer goods are purchased by people for personal and household use. Industrial goods are purchased by businesses and used in the production of consumer goods. These include the raw materials that go into the consumer goods, such as the wood that eventually becomes a rocking chair, and the machines used to produce the goods, such as the saw that cuts the wood. Consumer goods and industrial goods are distributed in different ways. We will focus mainly on consumer goods.

We will also look at how services distribution works. Services—from haircutting to data entry—are distributed from provider to consumer in many ways. When you buy a candy bar from your local convenience store or a pair of jeans from the mall, you are acting as a consumer. As a consumer, you form one end of a marketing channel, or channel of distribution. Your purchase of a product is the final step in a potentially long and complicated series of transactions. At the other end of the marketing channel is the manufacturer, or producer. The manufacturer makes the product, and you buy it.

What happens in between depends on the company and the type of product. Some products are well suited to direct sale by the manufacturer, while others have longer marketing channels. These longer marketing channels involve the flow of goods through middlemen, or inter-mediaries. Middlemen get goods from the manufacturer and pass them on to the consumer. A marketing channel can include more than one middleman. A marketing channel, then, is simply the route taken by products from their creation by the manufacturer to their purchase by the consumer: manufacturer ▶ middleman ▶ consumer.

Who are these middlemen, and why do they exist? There are two major types of middlemen: those who buy the goods and resell them, and those who simply pass the goods along without ever owning them. We say that the first kind takes title to the merchandise, whereas the second kind doesn't. Title simply means ownership.

Merchant middlemen take title. Some examples of merchant middlemen are wholesalers and retailers. Wholesalers and retailers buy goods and resell them at a

Fred the Middleman

Fred lives near a large food wholesaler, Big Foods, that is open to the public. Big Foods buys products directly from the manufacturer and sells products directly to consumers in bulk. Fred's family has a large garage, and his mother likes to save money by buying food in large quantities.

One day, Fred goes with his mother to Big Foods. He buys a lot of candy in bulk for a lot less than he would have paid at the convenience store. He decides to resell the candy to his friends at a profit.

Fred has become a middleman in the following marketing channel: Candy, Inc. (manufacturer) ▸ Big Foods (wholesaler) ▸ Fred (retailer) ▸ Fred's friends (Consumers). Does Fred take title to his merchandise? Yes; he buys the candy before selling it again.

What risks come with taking title to merchandise? Fred could have bought too much candy and found himself unable to sell it all. He might have bought the wrong kind of candy, or an unpopular flavor. Either way, he can't go back to Big Foods and return the candy for cash or credit. He has to sell all of his candy or spend the next few months eating it!

profit, on the way to the consumer. We will look at whole-salers and retailers more closely later.

Functional middlemen don't take title. Functional middlemen include agents, brokers, transporters, and public warehouses. Agents and brokers arrange sales by connecting buyers and sellers. They don't actually own the goods they move. Their profit usually comes in the form of a commission, paid by the buyer or seller of the goods. For instance, most people, when buying or selling a house, use a real estate agent. Real estate agents don't hold title to the houses they sell. They provide a service, connecting the right buyer with the right house. As payment for their service, they receive a commission, a percentage of the house's selling price.

Transporters and public warehouses are functional middlemen, too. They move goods from one place to another or store goods temporarily. They are paid for providing these functions, and the cost of these functions is usually added into the price the consumer pays for the product.

When you buy cheese and crackers from a vending machine, the price you pay might include agents' commissions, transportation and/or storage fees, and the profit margins of wholesalers and retailers. Cheese and Crackers, Inc., a food processor, might hire agents to arrange sales of their product to food wholesalers and distributors. The agents get a commission, of course. Food wholesalers and distributors, such as Super Foods, Inc., might sell the product to vending machine operators.

Super Foods takes a profit, of course. Vending machine operators, in turn, sell the product to you. They take a profit, too. Phew! Everywhere along the way, it seems, middlemen make things more expensive.

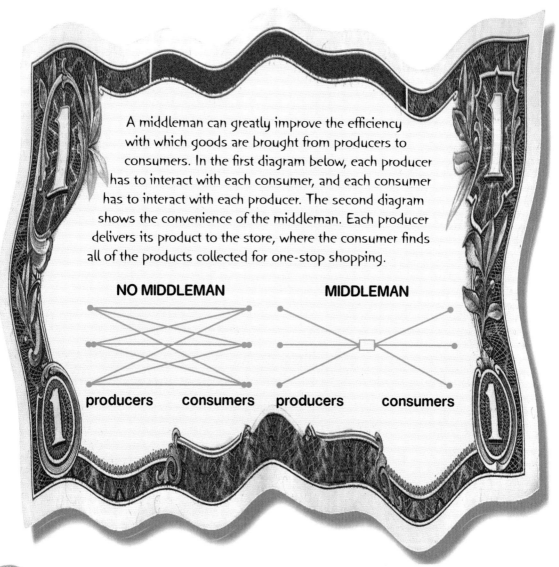

A middleman can greatly improve the efficiency with which goods are brought from producers to consumers. In the first diagram below, each producer has to interact with each consumer, and each consumer has to interact with each producer. The second diagram shows the convenience of the middleman. Each producer delivers its product to the store, where the consumer finds all of the products collected for one-stop shopping.

NO MIDDLEMAN

MIDDLEMAN

producers consumers producers consumers

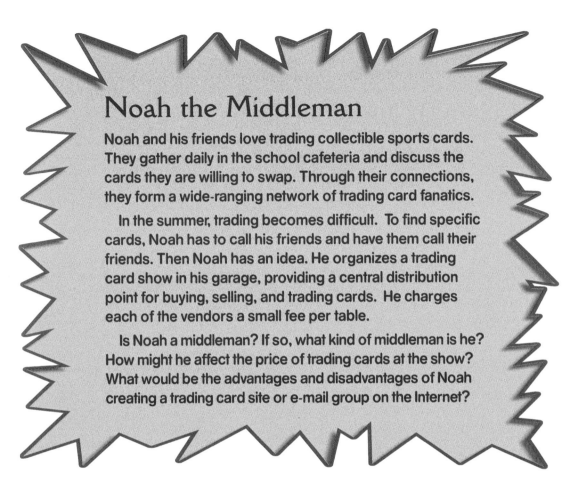

Noah the Middleman

Noah and his friends love trading collectible sports cards. They gather daily in the school cafeteria and discuss the cards they are willing to swap. Through their connections, they form a wide-ranging network of trading card fanatics.

In the summer, trading becomes difficult. To find specific cards, Noah has to call his friends and have them call their friends. Then Noah has an idea. He organizes a trading card show in his garage, providing a central distribution point for buying, selling, and trading cards. He charges each of the vendors a small fee per table.

Is Noah a middleman? If so, what kind of middleman is he? How might he affect the price of trading cards at the show? What would be the advantages and disadvantages of Noah creating a trading card site or e-mail group on the Internet?

A World Without Middlemen

Perhaps you've seen advertisements for discount outlets or open-to-the-public wholesalers: "We eliminate the middleman and pass the savings on to you!" Is eliminating the middleman a good idea? Not always. Most middlemen play vital roles in the marketing channel by efficiently delivering products from manufacturers to consumers. In a world with no middlemen, we would have to shop at a hundred different manufacturers. Or we would have manufacturers ringing our doorbells all day long to sell us

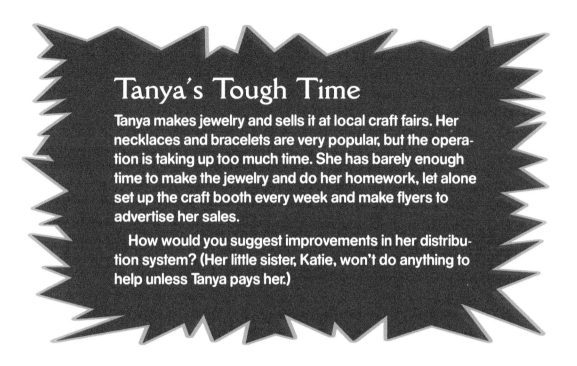

Tanya's Tough Time

Tanya makes jewelry and sells it at local craft fairs. Her necklaces and bracelets are very popular, but the operation is taking up too much time. She has barely enough time to make the jewelry and do her homework, let alone set up the craft booth every week and make flyers to advertise her sales.

How would you suggest improvements in her distribution system? (Her little sister, Katie, won't do anything to help unless Tanya pays her.)

their goods. There would be no department stores or convenience stores. Our choices would be severely limited.

Multiple Middlemen

Longer marketing channels (those with more middlemen) can actually prove more efficient than shorter ones. While more middlemen may mean a higher price for the consumer, it may also mean that a greater variety of products is available, or that products are more convenient to purchase. Would you drive fifty miles to pay $30 for a pair of jeans that are available for $32.50 around the corner? Would you want to walk to a bakery for bread, a dairy for milk, and a butcher for meat, or would you rather buy all three at a supermarket?

From the Manufacturer to You!

There are four typical marketing channels:

1. Manufacturer ▶ Consumer

This "direct sale" method seems like it would be the simplest and most logical. However, it does not prove practical for most consumer goods. Chewing gum is a good example. Large gum companies would not be very profitable if they tried to sell their product directly to consumers. Imagine a door-to-door gum salesman! Gum companies concentrate on what they know best: making gum. They use other companies to distribute and market their goods.

Some manufacturers sell directly to consumers over the Internet. Computer manufacturers, such as IBM and Compaq, have established on-line stores

through which customers can buy their products. Because on-line stores are fairly inexpensive to operate and can build customer loyalty, manufacturers of all kinds have begun to consider the on-line store option.

2. Manufacturer ▶ Retailer ▶ Consumer

This marketing channel is employed when a retailer is large enough to buy goods from the manufacturer. Big retail stores like Wal-Mart and Sears have large enough markets that they can purchase consumer goods directly from manufacturers and sell them to consumers, often at a discount. Automobiles are often sold in this way as well, through dealerships.

Some on-line shopping sites participate as middlemen in this marketing channel. They seek to attract consumers who want a wide variety of options and brands. While IBM's on-line store stocks only IBMs, an on-line retailer such as Egghead.com offers computers from many different manufacturers.

3. Manufacturer ▸ Wholesaler ▸ Retailer ▸ Consumer

This is probably the most common marketing channel for consumer goods. If a manufacturer wants to sell its product to thousands of consumers in hundreds of retail stores, it usually won't dedicate the time and energy required to sell to all of those retail stores, especially if the stores are spread across the country. The manufacturer will sell to a wholesaler, who will handle distribution to retail stores.

4. Manufacturer ▸ Agent Middleman ▸ Consumer

This channel is used by cosmetics companies like Mary Kay and Avon, as well as by Tupperware. The manufacturer enlists a large sales force of functional middlemen, who sell the product in their local area. The agent middlemen in this marketing channel do not take title to the products they sell and are paid a commission on their sales. Without the agent middleman, the manufacturer would find it difficult to sell to so many consumers.

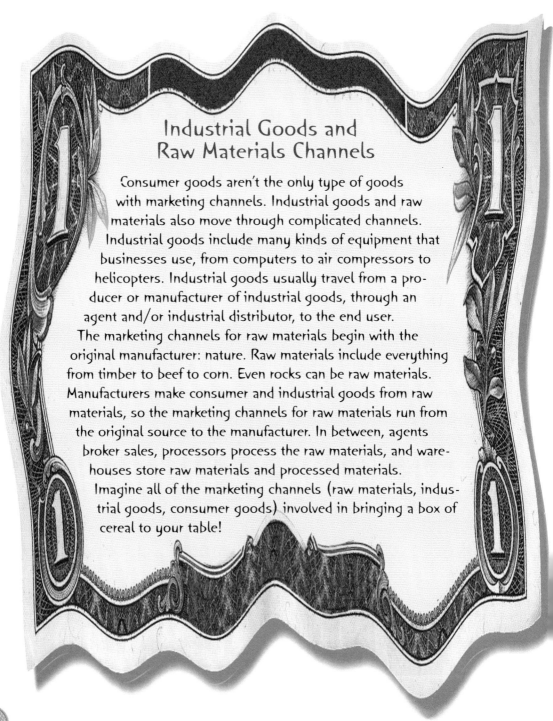

Industrial Goods and Raw Materials Channels

Consumer goods aren't the only type of goods with marketing channels. Industrial goods and raw materials also move through complicated channels. Industrial goods include many kinds of equipment that businesses use, from computers to air compressors to helicopters. Industrial goods usually travel from a producer or manufacturer of industrial goods, through an agent and/or industrial distributor, to the end user.

The marketing channels for raw materials begin with the original manufacturer: nature. Raw materials include everything from timber to beef to corn. Even rocks can be raw materials. Manufacturers make consumer and industrial goods from raw materials, so the marketing channels for raw materials run from the original source to the manufacturer. In between, agents broker sales, processors process the raw materials, and warehouses store raw materials and processed materials.

Imagine all of the marketing channels (raw materials, industrial goods, consumer goods) involved in bringing a box of cereal to your table!

Manny Millionaire's Gadget

Two years ago, Manny Millionaire invented a space-saving gadget for storing shoes in a closet. He started manufacturing his gadget and selling it through his friends and family around the country. He paid his friends and family a small amount for every gadget sold. He sold a lot of gadgets in the first year, but afterward, sales slowed down considerably. His friends and family couldn't find any new customers. They had sold the gadget to almost everyone they knew. The manufacturer-to-agent middleman-to-consumer marketing channel had dried up.

Manny knew that he had to change his marketing strategy to reach new customers. He devised three options:

1. Manufacturer ▸ Consumer. Manny considered selling his product directly to the consumer through an Internet site. The problem with this approach was that Manny's gadget had no brand identity—no one had ever heard of it. He would have difficulty attracting people to his Web site.

2. Manufacturer ▸ Wholesaler ▸ Retailer ▸ Consumer. Manny attempted to sell his product to a wholesaler, but the wholesaler wasn't interested in the gadget. Manny's gadget didn't belong in a large variety of retail stores.

3. Manufacturer ▸ Retailer ▸ Consumer. Finally, Manny contacted three nationwide specialty stores. Two were not interested in his gadget. They already carried similar products. The third, Space Saverz, liked his gadget and ordered a shipment of 10,000.

With the right marketing channel, a seemingly dead business can reach a new consumer base and grow.

Retailing

What's the difference between retailers and wholesalers? They're both middlemen, right? At first glance, the differences seem pretty simple: retailers sell directly to consumers, and wholesalers buy direct from the manufacturer. But can't wholesalers sell directly to the consumer? Discount bulk food stores sometimes do. And can't retailers buy directly from the manufacturer? Your local Ford dealer probably does.

Basically, retailers and wholesalers differ in their position in the marketing channel. Retailers are closer to the consumer, wholesalers are closer to the manufacturer. So when we talk about retail, we usually talk about the ways in which products are sold to customers.

What's Up with Product Lines?

Retailers can be classified according to the breadth and depth of their product lines. A product line is any number of closely related products manufactured by one company. Ford, for instance, might introduce improvements in their line of trucks or line of cars every year. A Schick product line might include reusable razors, blades, disposable razors, and shaving creams and gels. Products manufactured by two different companies are not in the same product line, and unrelated products made by one company probably aren't considered in the same product line, either.

A store's product lines are said to be narrow if the store does not offer a great variety of product lines. For instance, a store carrying only two brands of toothpaste has a fairly narrow range of product lines, whereas a store that carries a dozen brands of toothpaste is said to have a wide range of product lines.

Product lines themselves can be shallow or deep. A shallow product line might include only toothpaste and toothbrushes. A deeper product line would also include mouthwash, dental floss, and—yuck!—tongue scrapers.

Imagine that you want to buy a new outfit, but you're not sure what you're after. You'll want to go to a store with a wide variety of product lines, so you can see what various manufacturers have to offer. And once you have decided on a product line you like, you would like to see what else is available from within that product line. Can you guess what kind of store you're looking for? Here's a hint: While

you're shopping for clothes, your parents can shop for a new refrigerator, with several brands to choose from. Obviously, we're talking about a department store.

Department stores have a wide variety of product lines separated by category into different self-contained departments. Within each department, the product lines are deep. Nowadays, some department stores specialize in apparel and cosmetics, but there are still department stores, such as Sears, Roebuck and Co. or J.C. Penney, where one can buy everything from a blender to a pair of socks.

Mass merchandisers, such as discount stores and supermarkets, often carry product lines as wide or wider than department stores. In general, though, the product lines in such stores tend to be shallower. Supermarkets, for instance, don't automatically stock everything in a given product line. The computerized scanner at the checkout counter keeps track of sales and inventory, and products that don't sell are often replaced with those that do. Discount stores, such as Wal-Mart and Target, offer a wide variety of products at lower prices than conventional retailers. They're able to do this because they make less money per item. They're able to make less money per item because they have a higher sales volume than do traditional retailers.

What kind of store has a narrow assortment of deep product lines? Let's go shopping again. You know what kind of clothes you like, and you know who makes them. You're looking for a store that carries their entire line of products. Such stores are called specialty retailers. The Limited is a specialty retailer, as is Abercrombie & Fitch. Specialty retailers usually carry one kind of product, like clothing or housewares, by a limited number of manufacturers. By specializing in a few product lines, specialty retailers can stock more of each product line.

Why would anyone in his or her right mind want to run a retail store with a narrow assortment of shallow product lines? Does such a thing even exist? How about convenience stores, like 7-Eleven or Circle K? In a convenience store, you don't usually have as many choices.

That's because convenience store shoppers aren't necessarily looking for choice. They're looking for convenience. When you need a toothbrush right away, it doesn't matter if it's made by Reach or by Oral-B—a toothbrush is a toothbrush is a toothbrush!

As any young zillionaire knows, you don't need a store to sell stuff. There are as many varieties of non-store retailing as there are varieties of store. Businesses sell products and services to consumers door-to-door, through vending machines, through catalogs, and on the Internet.

Nonstore retailing has the advantage of being low-cost. If you don't have a store, you don't need to pay high rent for a high traffic location. However, nonstore retailers face a different challenge: reaching consumers in clever and innovative ways.

Product Lines

	WIDE ASSORTMENT	NARROW ASSORTMENT
DEEP PRODUCT LINES	Department Stores	Specialty Retailers
SHALLOW PRODUCT LINES	Discount Stores and Supermarkets	Convenience Stores

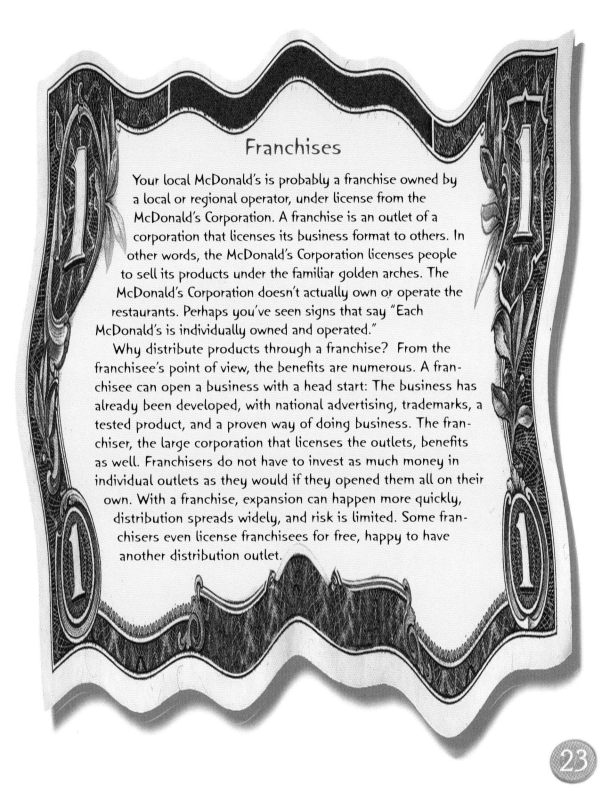

Franchises

Your local McDonald's is probably a franchise owned by a local or regional operator, under license from the McDonald's Corporation. A franchise is an outlet of a corporation that licenses its business format to others. In other words, the McDonald's Corporation licenses people to sell its products under the familiar golden arches. The McDonald's Corporation doesn't actually own or operate the restaurants. Perhaps you've seen signs that say "Each McDonald's is individually owned and operated."

Why distribute products through a franchise? From the franchisee's point of view, the benefits are numerous. A franchisee can open a business with a head start: The business has already been developed, with national advertising, trademarks, a tested product, and a proven way of doing business. The franchiser, the large corporation that licenses the outlets, benefits as well. Franchisers do not have to invest as much money in individual outlets as they would if they opened them all on their own. With a franchise, expansion can happen more quickly, distribution spreads widely, and risk is limited. Some franchisers even license franchisees for free, happy to have another distribution outlet.

A Retailer: To Be or Not to Be?

Would you like to own your own retail store? You'll need some money—perhaps a small business loan—but there are plenty of things to think about beforehand. Retailing requires a lot of strategic planning. First of all, you should consider whether or not a franchise is an option. Some people like the stability and developed consumer base that comes with a franchise. Others have their own vision of what they want their store to be.

What would you like to sell? Clothing? Computer games? Both? Your first decisions should focus on the breadth and depth of your product lines. Many small business entrepreneurs choose to start out with a specialty retail store, putting to work their passion for, let's say, aquarium fish. Do you have any hobbies that would translate well into a retail store?

Where would you like to locate your business? This is one of the most crucial decisions a retailer can make. Think about the kinds of customers you want to attract. An antique store that would prosper in a quaint town might fail in an urban mall. What about the rent you will have to pay, versus how profitable you expect your business to be? An aquarium fish store might fail in a mall because of high rent. However, the same store on a highway strip-mall could succeed. A greeting card store, on the other hand, is best placed where there is a lot of foot traffic.

What kind of services to you plan to offer your customers? Do you plan to hire salespeople? If you plan to start a restaurant, will it be table service or carry-out? What kind of image would you like your store to have? Is your store family-oriented or for teenagers only? If you'd like to start a clothing store or skateboard shop, perhaps you'll want your store to seem really cool and fun. However, if your idea is an environmentally friendly dry-cleaning service, you'll want the store to seem clean and businesslike.

Wholesaling

While retail functions have to do with the consumer, wholesale functions have more to do with manufacturers and other businesses. Wholesalers sell products and services to other businesses, at lower than retail price. Some products are resold by the businesses, other products are used by the businesses.

The Ins and Outs of Wholesaling

There are two major types of wholesaler: full-service and limited-service. Full-service wholesalers offer many convenient services to manufacturers and retailers. Limited-service wholesalers fulfill specific needs for manufacturers and retailers at a lower cost than full-service wholesalers. Full-service wholesalers often develop long-term relationships with their manufacturers and retailers. They stock inventory, operate warehouses, supply credit, employ sales-people, and deliver products to retailers. Limited-service wholesalers offer goods without many extra services. Cash-and-carry wholesalers, for instance, require cash payment for goods and don't provide transportation.

Connecting Retailers to Manufacturers

So what do full-service wholesalers do? Mainly, they make it easier for retailers and manufacturers to connect. Besides buying from manufacturers, wholesalers employ a sales force to inform and educate retailers about certain products. In other words, if XYZ Computers is going to launch a new laptop computer, their wholesaler will some-times help retailers become more familiar with the features of the new laptop.

Wholesalers can also sort manufactured goods for retailers or other wholesalers. This is especially important in food services. A large orange grower, for instance, could sell all of its oranges to a wholesaler, who could then decide which oranges would be good for juice and which ones would be good for the produce department of super-markets. If retailers purchased directly from the manufac-turer, either the retailer or the grower would have to sort through all of the oranges, which would keep them from doing what they do best: growing oranges, selling oranges, or making juice. Manufacturers tend to offer their products in large blocks, too big for most retailers to handle.

Wholesalers help out by dividing the large blocks among retailers and other businesses further down the marketing channel. They also assume the risks of storing and transporting the goods.

Finally, wholesalers can offer retailers credit or financing, which allows retailers to buy more goods on the expectation that they will be able to sell them. If a retailer wants to buy a million dollars worth of clothes and expects to sell at least two-thirds of those clothes at a profit, the retailer does not need to pay the wholesaler the whole million dollars. The wholesaler lends the retailer the clothes and waits until the retailer has sold some before collecting the money.

Planes, Trains, Trucks, and Boats

How do goods actually get from one place to another, and who decides how much goes where? At the core of all goods distribution lies physical distribution, or business logistics. Business logistics includes order processing, materials handling, warehousing, inventory, and transportation. On average, over 20 percent of the cost of products in our economy comes from physical distribution costs. In other words, for an average $100 item, $20 of its cost comes from tracking, storage, and transport.

Transporting Goods

Take a look at the labels on your clothes. Where were your clothes manufactured? Honduras? Thailand? Mexico? Hong Kong? Most of your clothes were probably made somewhere outside the United States. But did you go to Thailand to buy your pants? Probably not. You probably bought your pants in a local store. Why do you think your pants came all the way from Thailand? Wouldn't it make more sense to manufacture them in the United States, closer to the store? Maybe, except that labor is much cheaper in other countries, and the cost of shipping is less than the difference in labor cost. In other words, cheap worldwide transportation makes cheap labor available to companies based here in the United States.

The same goes for raw materials. Manufacturers can obtain raw materials from around the globe, ship them to manufacturing centers where labor is cheap, and ship the final products to the United States, where consumers will pay top dollar.

Transportation makes resources available, which then allows for specialization.

Specialization means that each geographic region does not have to produce all the materials it requires. Instead, a region might specialize in coal mining, while another specializes in textile manufacturing. Thanks to efficient transportation networks, manufacturers in just about any region can get the materials they need from other regions.

Distribution channels often require a significant amount of transportation. Let's look at the distribution and marketing channel for a consumer good, say, a dining room chair:

Raw Materials ▸ Processor ▸ Manufacturer ▸ Wholesaler ▸ Retailer ▸ Consumer

Timber ▸ Lumber Mill ▸ J.J. Furniture ▸ Home Products, Inc. ▸ Home-Mart ▸ You

The distribution and marketing channel requires up to five separate transports, not to mention storage and tracking. That's a lot of mileage. Even if you're buying a chair from a local craftsman, the channel still looks pretty long:

Timber ▸ Lumber Mill ▸ Manufacturer ▸ You

It's easy to see how logistical costs can add up to at least 20 percent of a product's final price!

Transportation decisions can mean the success or failure of any business that deals with goods. You wouldn't ship a carton of kiwis the same way you would ship a carton of shoes, would you? Why not? Kiwis go bad! Kiwis have to be sent more quickly than shoes. Why not send shoes just as quickly? It costs too much!

The Major Modes of Transport

The major modes of transport for goods today include planes, trains, trucks, and boats. They can be organized according to their characteristics.

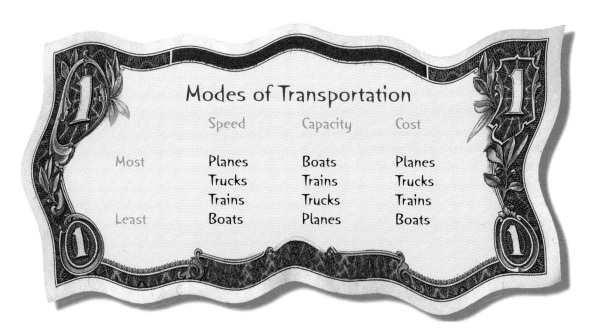

Modes of Transportation			
	Speed	Capacity	Cost
Most	Planes	Boats	Planes
	Trucks	Trains	Trucks
	Trains	Trucks	Trains
Least	Boats	Planes	Boats

As you can see, choosing which mode of transport to use is a pretty complicated process. For instance, if you need to send a shipment of lumber from Seattle to Los Angeles, you could use any of the four modes of transport. Which one do you think would be most efficient? You probably wouldn't send your shipment by plane because air transport has the least capacity and the highest cost, and you don't need to get the lumber to Los Angeles overnight! That leaves trucks, trains, and boats. Now the decision-making process becomes even more complicated. How soon does the lumber have to be in Los Angeles? A rush order might go by truck, though that could end up costing a lot. Is the company trying to keep physical distribution costs to a minimum? Then boats may be the solution because shipping over water is the least expensive, though the slowest. Transporting the lumber by train might be the solution if the company doesn't mind paying a little more to get their lumber more quickly. In any case, you can be sure that these costs of distribution will end up in the price of the final product!

Services Are Distributed, Too

Rex the Bow-Wow's Party

Zoltan the Zillionaire wants to throw a party for his pooch, Rex, but he doesn't have time to call the DJ, the caterer, and the pooper-scooper. So Zoltan calls Peter's Party Planners. When someone calls Peter for a party, Pete schedules a time to talk about all of the details. Peter is a middleman in a marketing channel that involves no exchange of goods. He is a broker of services. He connects the consumer, in this case Zoltan, to service providers, such as the DJ and caterer.

Peter can get discounts on rented ballrooms and restaurants. Thanks to the relationships he has developed with other party-oriented businesses, Peter can offer a complete package at a competitive price—not much more than Zoltan would pay if he called everyone on his own.

Of course, money is no object to Zoltan. He is, after all, throwing a party for his dog!

What's the Deal with Services, Anyway?

What are services? How are they different from goods? Services are things people and businesses do for other people and businesses. Some examples of services include haircuts, dry cleaning, and airline travel. You can't hold services in your hand. They are intangible.

Many small business ideas for kids are service-based, simply because service-based businesses don't necessarily require a lot of money to start up. You don't have to manufacture a product to be a dog walker, a baby-sitter, or a landscaper. You simply have to have the right equipment and be willing to work hard. Most services are distributed directly, from the service provider to the customer. When you agree to baby-sit the Miller boys on Friday night, you do not contact a baby-sitting distributor; you show up on Friday night and baby-sit them yourself!

So if services are intangible and often marketed directly, how can services be distributed? Simple: Some services have longer marketing channels. Intermediaries connect the service provider to the consumer. Can you think of any services offered through an intermediary agent?

How about airline travel? You can buy airline tickets directly from the airline, but many people prefer to use a travel agent. Why? Remember the middleman diagram? If you want to compare prices for a trip from Los Angeles to New York, calling one travel agent is easier than calling a dozen airlines individually.

Dry cleaning is another example. Some dry cleaners have signs that say "Plant on Premises," meaning that they perform the dry cleaning themselves. These dry cleaners participate in a direct marketing channel. However, many dry cleaners send your clothes to a separate plant for cleaning. In this case, the dry cleaner you visit is acting as an intermediary between you and the service provider.

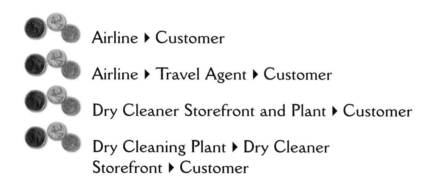

Airline ▸ Customer

Airline ▸ Travel Agent ▸ Customer

Dry Cleaner Storefront and Plant ▸ Customer

Dry Cleaning Plant ▸ Dry Cleaner Storefront ▸ Customer

In distributing or marketing services, some decisions have to be made, depending on the type of service to be provided and the number of customers to be served. First, a location has to be established. Location is crucial for some service businesses, such as haircutters and manicurists, who usually provide their services at their place of business. These businesses thrive in areas with a lot of foot traffic, such as large shopping malls. Other service businesses, such as telephone and Internet service providers, can be located almost anywhere.

Brad Gets Into the Business of Supplying a Service

Brad is a computer whiz. He knows more about computers than anyone in his class. Recently, his parents bought a new computer and asked Brad to show them how to use it. He was shocked at how little they knew about computers. His father took a free computer class offered through the manufacturer and invited Brad along. No one in the class knew anything about computers either. That's when Brad decided to offer classes of his own.

Before launching his business, though, Brad had to make some important decisions. Would he invite a group of people to his house or go to other people's houses? Would he do all the teaching, or would he hire one of his whiz-kid friends to help? Would he design his own textbook or use an existing one? Would he provide a computer hotline for his students? How much would he charge? Would he offer a money-back guarantee? All of these are questions of services distribution or services marketing. The answers depend on how big Brad wants his business to become, how many customers he thinks he can handle, how hard he wants to work, and whether he can realistically compete with other similar services in his area.

Brad decided to start small. He charges an hourly rate for one-on-one instruction. Most of the local classes, through manufacturers and colleges, don't offer one-on-one tutoring, so Brad's business is not in direct competition with them. Brad gives his students a simple textbook that he designed and copied himself. He works five to ten hours a week and depends mainly on the recommendation of current students for new business.

Brad's sister, Linda, has decided to get in on the act. She is going to baby-sit Brad's students' kids while Brad teaches their parents!

Second, a service business needs to decide whether or not it will provide pick-up and delivery. Some dry cleaners will come to your house and pick up your clothes, returning them a few days later. Maid services have to come to your house to clean it. Your parents can take a car to the car wash or call someone to come to your house and wash it.

Third, a service business needs to figure out if there will be a marketing channel, or if the service will be marketed directly. In other words, will the customer and service provider interact directly, or will the customer enlist services through an intermediary? Airlines market their services both ways, directly and through travel agents. Your parents might hire a baby-sitter directly or contact one through a baby-sitting service.

Finally, a service business needs to determine what kind of supplies it will require to conduct business. An airline needs lots of supplies: airplanes, luggage carts, computers, food and beverages for the passengers. A baby-sitter needs few, if any, supplies.

The Nature of Distributing Services

The high-tech information revolution has transformed the nature of many service-oriented businesses. Thanks to the Internet, location is not as crucial a factor for many businesses. As long as information sent over the Internet can be encrypted, or put into code so no one can read it, information-based businesses can locate themselves almost anywhere.

This has led to a phenomenon called outsourcing. In outsourcing, a company hires another company to take care of some of its work. For instance, if a doctor is finding it too expensive to hire a full-time employee to type reports, the doctor might use an outsourcing firm to type his reports. Then, he pays only for the service when he needs it, instead of having to hire someone full-time. Similarly, a large corporation might hire a separate company to handle its customer service calls or complaint lines.

Worldwide communication has resulted in outsourcing to other countries, where the labor is cheaper. India, for instance, has many outsourcing firms. Some companies find it more economical to outsource customer service or data entry to India than to pay employees in Europe or North America.

The Internet has also spurred growth in some unique service businesses, such as information brokers. Information brokers provide answers to questions like: Who owns a specific piece of property? How are my competitors doing? or How is the umbrella market in Nairobi? Information brokers provide their service to other businesses for a fee, but the Internet is full of fun sites providing a watered-down version of the service for free. Sites like askanexpert.com let you pose questions to experts. These sites function as intermediaries, linking you with a volunteer service provider.

Did you know that education is a service? Traditionally, distribution of this service has been limited by the location of the school. Aside from a few correspondence, or learn-by-mail, programs, students have had to go to school in order to graduate and earn a degree. Now, thanks to new technology, some universities and colleges offer off-campus degrees, extending the reach of their services beyond their original locations. You can take classes by correspondence, videotape, or through the Internet.

Distribution and marketing of services is in transition, thanks to new technologies, and starting up a service-oriented business has never been easier. The trick, as it has always been, is reaching customers.

The Internet Is Changing Everything

Many companies that have been successful in the real world are now looking to eliminate the middleman by selling their products on-line. Now that you know more about distribution and the many important services middlemen provide, can you imagine the risks and dangers of eliminating the middleman in the following businesses?

- Book Publishing
- Music Stores
- Grocery Stores
- Auction Houses

Getting Rid of the Middlemen

People who used to have to get their books published by big publishing companies and then distributed by book distributors can now publish and distribute their books on the Internet. What are the dangers of eliminating all of the middlemen (agents, editors, publishers, promoters) in this process? Without anyone else to read or edit the book before it reaches the marketplace, quality can suffer. The Internet is full of low-quality self-published writing. Do you think this will always be the case, or do you think that quality electronic publishing will someday emerge?

Do you know what an MP3 is? It's a music format for the Internet that sounds almost as good as a CD. It's easy to record, too, and the files are small enough to make them easy to download. MP3s and other electronic music formats have created a revolution in how some music gets distributed. Rock bands don't need to sign with big record labels anymore—all they need is a Web site! Their costs are kept low, and their profits, if people are willing to pay to download their songs, don't have to be split with any middlemen. The major challenge is promotion. Eliminating the middleman also eliminates the services provided by the middleman, and one of those services is the ability to attract consumers to the product. So, while a rock group's Web site provides potential access to many consumers, it does not guarantee that consumers will buy the product.

Ulrich's Brainy Idea

Woody had a dozen CDs he never listened to anymore, so he took them to his local used record store to sell them for credit. The record store offered him $4 in credit for each CD he returned. He had bought the CDs new for almost $15 each, but he made the deal anyway. It was better to have $48 in credit at the record store than a dozen CDs he never listened to.

A few days later, Woody visited the store again. As he looked through the used CDs, he saw in the racks one of the CDs he had returned. The price, to his amazement, was marked at $8.99!

"Hey," he said to the man behind the counter, "how come you paid me only $4 when I traded in this CD?"

The shaggy-haired man behind the counter shrugged his shoulders. "That's business, kid."

Yes, it was business. The record store had to cover the cost of storing the CD, including the possibility that no one might ever buy it. More than that, though, the store took advantage of its position as a known retail outlet. It had an established channel of distribution to consumers. If Woody had tried to sell his CDs on the street, he probably wouldn't have had much luck. He wouldn't have had enough selection to attract customers.

Ulrich had a dozen CDs, too. But instead of selling his CDs back to a record store, he sold them on an Internet auction site. He sold ten CDs for $6 each, and the buyers paid for the shipping. The buyers were happy to buy used CDs for less than $8.99. Two of Ulrich's CDs didn't sell, and he took those to the used record store and received credit for them. By taking distribution into his own hands, Ulrich ended up with $60 in cash, plus $8 in store credit!

You can buy groceries on-line! On-line grocery stores, like Peapod, let you order your groceries on-line. They deliver right to your door! Peapod is available only in certain cities, but the idea could spread quickly. Although the on-line grocery store does not necessarily eliminate many middlemen, it is more convenient for the consumer who does not want to spend time at the supermarket. Peapod's original distribution system was primitive: They would go to regular grocery stores and buy the products off the shelves when customers ordered them. They operated as personal shoppers. Now, however, Peapod has streamlined their distribution chain and gets their food from wholesalers, which increases their profits. A service-oriented business (grocery delivery service) became a retailer (grocery store) with premium services (on-line ordering, delivery).

On-line auctions are also revolutionizing distribution. People who never before had access to distribution are suddenly finding ways to reach thousands of potential customers. And what are they doing with this new power? Selling their junk!

The Internet is a wild and messy web of connections, in which any manufacturer or producer can be connected directly to any consumer, without a middleman or extended marketing channel. Do you think the Internet will stay this way, or do you think that marketing channels will develop as the Internet gets more mature? One thing is for sure: The Internet has already revolutionized the way we look at distributing goods and services.

GLOSSARY

commission Fee paid to an agent or broker for making a sale, usually a percentage of the selling price.

encrypted Put into code so that outsiders cannot read it.

entrepreneur Someone who starts his or her own business.

franchise Company, like McDonald's, that allows others to use its business format to better market its products.

functional middleman Middleman, such as an agent or a broker, that does not own the goods he or she deals with.

intangible Not able to be touched or possessed.

marketing channel Path taken by goods or services from the manufacturer or provider to the consumer.

merchant middleman Middleman that owns the goods he or she deals with.

middleman Any business or individual in the marketing channel between the manufacturer and the consumer.

outsourcing Practice of hiring outside companies to handle jobs that used to be done by employees.

physical distribution The sorting, storing, and transport of goods.

title A piece of paper that proves ownership of something.

FOR MORE INFORMATION

Foundation for Teaching Economics
http://www.fte.org

Future Business Leaders of America
http://www.fbla-pbl.org

Junior Achievement
http://www.ja.org

Moneyopolis
http://www.moneyopolis.com

***Time* for Kids**
http://www.pathfinder.com/TFK

United States Congress Joint Economic Committee
http://www.senate.gov/~jec

United States Department of Commerce Bureau of Economic Analysis
http://www.bea.doc.gov

***Zillions* Magazine**
http://www.zillionsedcenter.org

FOR FURTHER READING

Bangs, David H., Jr., and Linda Pinson. *The Real World Entrepreneur Field Guide*. New York: Upstart Press, 1999.

The Economist Guide to Economic Indicators: Making Sense of Economics. New York: John Wiley & Sons, 1997.

Giesbrecht, Martin Gerhard, and Gary E. Clayton. *A Guide to Everyday Economic Thinking*. New York: McGraw-Hill, 1997.

Godfrey, Neale S. *Neale S. Godfrey's Ultimate Kids' Money Book*. New York: Simon & Schuster, 1998.

Heilbroner, Robert, and Lester Thurow. *Economics Explained*. New York: Simon & Schuster, 1994.

Modu, Emmanuel. *The Lemonade Stand: A Guide to Encouraging the Entrepreneur in Your Child*. Newark, NJ: Gateway Publishers, 1996.

Otfinoski, Steven. *The Kid's Guide to Money: Earning It, Saving It, Spending It, Growing It, Sharing It*. New York: Scholastic, 1996.

Roper, Ingrid. *Moneymakers: Good Cents for Girls*. Middleton, WI: Pleasant Company Publications, 1998.

INDEX

CREDITS

About the Author

Antoine Wilson is a freelance writer living in Eastern Iowa.

Photo Credits

Cover photos © Artville; p. 6 © Gail Mooney/Corbis; p. 14 © Kelly-Mooney Photography/Corbis; p. 20 © Campbell-Boulanger/FPG; p. 27 © W. Metzen/H. Armstrong Roberts, Inc.; p. 29 © Allan H. Shoemake/FPG; p. 39 © Henk Tukker/International Stock.

Series Design
Law Alsobrook

Layout
Cynthia Williamson